# THE
# KENNET & AVON
# CANAL

*The Seal of The Kennet and Avon Canal Co.*

# THE
# KENNET & AVON CANAL

Clive & Helen Hackford
for The Kennet & Avon Canal Trust

TEMPUS

First published 2001
Copyright © Clive and Helen Hackford  2001

Tempus Publishing Limited
The Mill, Brimscombe Port,
Stroud, Gloucestershire, GL5 2QG
www.tempus-publishing.com

ISBN 0 7524 2129 8

Typesetting and origination by
Tempus Publishing Limited
Printed in Great Britain by
Midway Colour Print, Wiltshire

# Foreword

Looking at the Kennet and Avon Canal today we see a beautiful, bustling waterway where a wide variety of leisure interests are enjoyed; there are boats, fishermen, walkers, cyclists and naturalists. It is easy to forget the ups and downs in the fortunes of the canal. One hundred and ninety years ago it was a thriving commercial venture, but then came the railways which took away much of the trade and the canal's prosperity declined. It fell into disuse, yet the actions of enthusiastic volunteers ensured that it did not die. The Kennet & Avon Canal Trust was eventually formed, dedicated to its restoration and promotion for leisure and appropriate commerce. The Lord Methuen was the first president of the Kennet & Avon Canal Association (which would later become the trust) and he spoke regarding the canal on several occasions in the House of Lords. Subsequently there have been a number of well-known presidents and chairmen, with General Sir Hugh Stockwell and Admiral Sir William O'Brien the best remembered today. Without their drive the canal might never have been rescued.

A partnership has developed between British Waterways, local communities and the trust. Together these organisations continue to pool resources to ensure that never again will this waterway come under threat of closure.

During my years as chairman of the Parliamentary Waterways Group, I was able to bear witness to the enthusiasm and commitment of all those involved in bringing this waterway back to a vibrant life. I welcomed the opportunity to be involved when invited to become president of The Kennet & Avon Canal Trust.

This book draws upon images from the Trust's archive of documents and photographs to present as far as possible a visual account of the canal's past.

Sir Anthony Durant
President, Kennet & Avon Canal Trust

4

# Contents

Forword     4

Introduction     7

1.     Bristol to Brassknocker Wharf (Avon)     15

2.     Brassknocker Wharf to Froxfield Wharf (Wiltshire)     43

3.     Froxfield Wharf to The Thames (Berkshire)     47

Acknowledgements     128

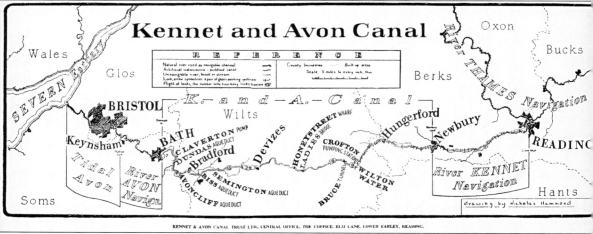

*The Kennet & Avon Canal showing the River Avon Navigation, the canal cut from Bath to Newbury and the River Kennet Navigation.*

# Introduction

It had long been a dream of traders and entrepreneurs to link the two major ports of Bristol and London by an inland waterway route. The link by sea was hazardous; exposure to Atlantic storms made Cornwall's coastline a graveyard for shipping and a succession of conflicts involving France made our ships in the English Channel ready prey for privateers.

Thus in 1788, a group of businessmen met in Hungerford and in a series of meetings agreed to form a committee to test public support for a scheme to connect the existing Avon and Kennet Navigations by an artificial cut from Newbury to Bath. Charles Dundas MP of Barton Court, Kintbury was elected chairman and Messrs Barnes, Simcock & Weston were commissioned to carry out a survey. They found no shortage of water on a route via Marlborough, Lacock, Melksham and Bradford-on-Avon. There was no lack of support either, and in 1791 John Rennie was asked to carry out a second survey. Rennie, reporting directly to

the committee, agreed with the earlier findings. Commissions were taken but it was agreed not to commence construction until £75,000 had been raised. Nearly two years had passed when a group of Bristol businessmen became impatient and decided to try to take over the Canal Committee. It had become clear that there was no problem raising the money and an agreement with the Canal Committee was quickly reached.

John Rennie was commissioned to carry out a third survey of the route, reporting back through Robert Whitworth, the committee's engineer. This time Rennie found a lack of water on the Marlborough route and recommended a new route via Devizes. Waylen, writing his *Chronicle of The Devizes* in 1839 tells us that this was brought about as a result of lobbying by the two Devizes MPs at the time, the Rt Hon. Henry Addington MP and Rt Hon. Joshua Smith MP.

# WESTERN CANAL.

**MARLBOROUGH, 29th July, 1788.**

AT a Meeting of the Committee appointed to take the Opinion of the Public, refpecting an Extenfion of the Navigation of the Rivers Kennett and Avon, fo as to form a direct Inland Communication between *London* and *Briftol*, and the Weft of *England*, by a Canal from *Newbury* to *Bath*,

## CHARLES DUNDAS, Efq. in the Chair,

RESOLVED, That a General Meeting be advertized to be held at the Caftle Inn, at Marlborough, Wilts, on *Tuefday* the 9th Day of *September* next, at Twelve o'Clock, at which Meeting the Landowners, and Parties interefted, are requefted to attend.

RESOLVED alfo, That the following Propofitions be fubmitted to the Opinion of that Meeting, *viz.*

1. That the Junction of the Kennett and Avon Rivers will be of Advantage to the Country.

2. That the under-named Gentlemen be propofed to the General Meeting as a Committee to regulate future Proceedings:

| | | |
|---|---|---|
| The Marquis of Lanfdown, | Matthew Humphries, | |
| The Earl of Ailefbury, | Andrew Bayntun, | |
| Lord Craven, | John Awdry, | |
| Lord Porchefter, | Paul Methuen, | |
| Sir Edward Bayntun, Bart. | Paul Cobb Methuen, | |
| John Awdry, | James Montagu, | |
| William Brummelle, | James Montagu, jun. | Efquires ; |
| William Pulteney, | Samuel Cam, | |
| John Walker Heneage, | Jofeph Mortimer, | |
| Lovelace Bigg, | ——— Dickenfon, | |
| John Pearce, } Efquires ; | Francis Page, | |
| ——— James, | John Baverftock, | |
| Charles Dundas, | John Ward | |
| Arthur Jones, | R. H. Gaby, | |
| Ifaac Pickering, | ——— Deane, | |
| John Hyde, | ——— Vanderflighen, | |

The Members for the Counties of Wilts, Berks, and Somerfet ; the Members for the feveral Boroughs in the faid Counties ; the Chief Magiftrates of the faid Boroughs ; and fuch other Perfons as fhall be propofed and approved of at the General Meeting.

3. That fuch Committee be directed to employ Mr. Whitworth, or fome other experienced Surveyor, to examine the different Tracts by which the Navigation may be carried, and to make his Report to the faid Committee.

*Charles Dundas*

---

The estimated cost was £330,000 and the bill put before Parliament became the Kennet and Avon Canal Act on 17 April 1794. Rennie became consulting engineer to the committee and advised that a broad canal be built. William Jessop was consulted and in a report of July 1794 largely agreed with Rennie's proposals but suggested a number of route changes, recommending a summit route slightly to the north. This avoided the need for a tunnel of more than two miles in length, thus saving in both construction time and money. It did, however, require water to be pumped to a much shorter two and a half-mile summit pound necessitating six extra locks '…of eight feet rise each…' and a length of deep cutting. Thus the need for Crofton pumping station and the reservoir of Wilton Water was born .

A N

# A C T

F O R

Making a Navigable Canal from the River *Kennet*, at or near the Town of *Newbury*, in the County of *Berks*, to the River *Avon*, at or near the City of *Bath*; and also certain Navigable Cuts therein described.

**WHEREAS** the making and maintaining of a Navigable Canal for Boats, Barges, and other Veſſels, from the River *Kennet*, at or near the Town of *Newbury*, in the County of *Berks*, to the River *Avon*, at or near the City of *Bath*, and also certain Navigable Cuts hereinafter deſcribed will greatly facilitate, and render more convenient and leſs expenſive than at preſent, the Conveyance of all Kinds of Commodities, not only to and from the ſeveral Towns and Places near the Lines of ſuch Canal and Cuts, but alſo to and from the Ports of *London* and *Briſtol*, and will be of great public Utility; but ſuch Canal and Cuts cannot be made without the Authority of Parliament:

The initial share issue was well subscribed and work started on construction of the canal at Bradford on Avon and Newbury at about the same time in October 1794. The management structure was not ideal. Delegated financial and work approval responsibilities resulted in payment for substandard work, which had to be redone, and even occasionally for work which had not been done at all. Rennie wanted to use more brick, but the vested interests in stone quarries of some of the proprietors meant that he was overruled in favour of Bath stone. Unquestionably, however, Rennie's architectural masterpiece, the Dundas aqueduct in the Bath valley, would have been impossible in brick. The last part of the canal to be completed was the Devizes flight of twenty-nine locks. The canal was opened for full navigation on 28 December 1810. There was no ceremony, for sections had been put to use as they were completed, with trans-shipment around the Devizes flight of locks.

The River Kennet Navigation was purchased in 1813, control of the Avon Navigation having been gained in 1796. This brought the total cost of the canal to a little over £979,000. Improvements were made to the two river navigations, making the total length of the canal (waterway) eighty-seven and a half miles from Hanham Lock, near Bristol, to High Bridge, Reading. As the canal came into use both the tonnage carried and the toll charges gradually rose. The Somerset Coal Canal and the Wilts and Berks Canals had been completed at about the same time as the Kennet and Avon. The latter was to benefit greatly from trade in coal from the Somerset coalfields and the opening up of Wiltshire trade on the Wilts and Berks, with its more northerly link to the Thames from Semington to Abingdon and beyond.

Trade via the Thames, though, was regularly interrupted when it was in flood. On 4 October 1819 a notice appeared in *The Morning Chronicle* calling a special meeting of the canal proprietors. They were to discuss submission of a plan to Parliament for the building of a canal from the Thames at Maidenhead to the Grand Junction Canal at Cowley, with a branch to the Thames at Windsor. Rennie had surveyed the route in 1815 and the Western Union Canal Bill, as it became known, passed its second reading despite objections. However, it was withdrawn in July 1820 as a result of objections at the committee stage. The canal was never built.

As with other canals the advent of the railways caused a loss of trade. A peak was reached around 1840 as a result of carrying railway construction materials. Matters came to a head eventually when the canal company proposed to build a railway of its own (The London Newbury & Bath Direct Railway) alongside the canal, and introduced a bill into Parliament. After the second reading a Parliamentary Select Committee sat to review a cluster of railway bills in the south and this led to a takeover of the Kennet & Avon Canal Co. by The Great Western Railway Co. (GWR) in 1852. As part of the conditions embodied in the agreement, GWR had to take over the Canal Co.'s liabilities and maintain the canal. The maintenance requirement was further reinforced for all railway companies that had gained control of canals, by section 17 of the Regulation of Railways Act of 1873.

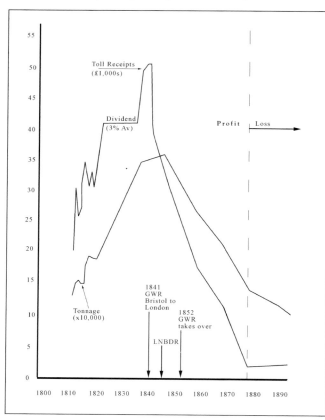

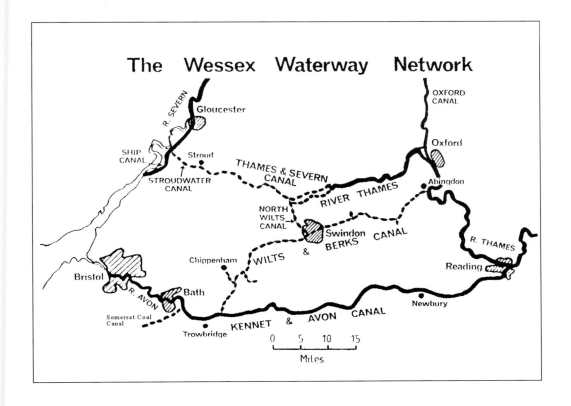

The Wessex Waterway Network

KENNET and AVON CANAL NAVIGA-
TION.—In pursuance of an Order of the Committee of
Management of the Affairs and Business of the Company of
Proprietors of the Kennet and Avon Canal Navigation, we do
hereby give notice, that a SPECIAL MEETING of the said
COMPANY of PROPRIETORS will be held at the City of
London Tavern, in Bishopsgate-street, London, on Wednesday
the 13th day of October next, at eleven o'clock in the forenoon,
to take into consideration a plan proposed to be submitted to
Parliament in the next Session for making a Navigable Canal
from the River Thames, near Maidenhead, in the County of
Berks, to the Grand Junction Canal, near Cowley, in the County of Middlesex, with a branch from the same into the River
Thames, near Windsor; and also to consider and determine
whether any and what assistance, by way of subscription or
otherwise, shall be given by the said Company in promoting
the said measure.

WARD and MERRIMAN, Principal Clerks.
Marlborough, Sept 21, 1819.

11

# LONDON, NEWBURY, AND BATH DIRECT RAILWAY,

## IN CONJUNCTION WITH THE KENNET AND AVON CANAL COMPANY.

SHARES *20*  DEPOSIT £ *30*

OFFICES OF THE COMPANY,
41, *Charing Cross, London, 8th October,* 1845.

SIR,

WE are instructed to inform you, in accordance with your request, that the COMMITTEE OF MANAGEMENT have allotted to you *20* SHARES of £15 each in respect of your present Shares in the KENNET AND AVON CANAL NAVIGATION, on condition that you pay the Deposit upon them of £1 10s. per Share, amounting to £ *30* .. .. .. on or before Tuesday, the 21st day of October instant, to one of the following Bankers, who will sign the receipt at the foot hereof. Unless the Deposit be paid by the day above named, the Shares will be forfeited.

MESSRS. ROBARTS, CURTIS, AND CO...LONDON.
MESSRS. MILES, HARFORD, AND CO...BRISTOL.
MESSRS. TUGWELL AND CO. .........BATH.
MESSRS. WARD AND CO. ..............MARLBOROUGH.

I beg also to inform you, that SCRIP CERTIFICATES for the above number of Shares will be delivered to you in exchange for this Letter, and the Banker's Receipt for the Deposit, after the execution of the Parliamentary Contract, &c. of which due notice will be given.

Be pleased to observe, that this Letter entire, with the Banker's Receipt, must be produced when you attend to execute the Deeds.

We are,
Your very obedient Servants,

*M. W. Merriman*

To *Miss Elizth. Weir*
*5 Lichfield Place*
*Clifton*

No. *36* _____ *16* October, 1845.

RECEIVED *for the Committee of Management of the* LONDON, NEWBURY, AND BATH DIRECT RAILWAY, *promoted by the* KENNET AND AVON CANAL COMPANY, *the sum of* *Thirty* Pounds, .. .. _____ *Shillings, to account for on Demand.*

£ *30*

The last year of profit was 1877, but GWR continued to maintain the canal in (barely) navigable condition until nationalisation in January 1948. Deterioration immediately set in, resulting in an illegal closure by the Docks & Inland Waterways Executive (DIWE). This resulted in the formation of the Kennet & Avon Canal Association (later Trust). In 1955 The British Transport Commission (BTC) tried to close the canal but John Gould, a canal carrier of Newbury who was unable to continue with his business, took DIWE to court. An out of court settlement of damages was made. This action marked the start of a campaign to reopen the Canal.

A petition to HM The Queen stirred Parliament into action. In 1956 the House of Commons refused to allow the canal to be closed and a committee under Mr Leslie Bowes was formed to investigate the future of canals. Mr R. Meinertzhagen formed the Kennet Carrying Co. and was able to demonstrate continued use of the Canal by resuming cruises from Reading to Burghfield Lock. In 1958 The Bowes Report was published, which classified canals and reprieved the Kennet & Avon. Eventually the British Waterways Board (BWB) was formed (later British Waterways) and relations between the trust and BWB rapidly advanced to one of total co-operation. The Riparian Local Government Authorities recognised the amenity value of the waterway and were most supportive. The canal was reopened to navigation by HM The Queen on 10 August 1990.

**A PUBLIC**

# PROTEST MEETING

AGAINST THE PROPOSED CLOSING OF THE

## KENNET & AVON CANAL

Will be Held at

## THE TOWN HALL, READING

FRIDAY, 25th NOVEMBER 1955 AT 7.30 P.M.

SPEAKERS:

## VISCOUNT SIDMOUTH
(President of the Kennet & Avon Canal Association)

## LESLIE MORTON, Esq. A.M. Inst. T.
(General Manager, Willow Wren Canal Carrying Co. Ltd)

## CAPT. L. R. MONK
(Managing Director 'Maid Line' Cruisers Ltd)

A Reading Branch of the **KENNET & AVON CANAL** Association will be formed, so **COME ALONG** and **SUPPORT THIS MEETING.** IN YOUR OWN INTEREST

FURTHER PARTICULARS FROM: D. D. HUTCHINGS, 'THE COPPICE' ELM LANE, LOWER EARLEY, READING.

---

### THE POLITICAL CALENDAR

1948  AS PART OF RAILWAY NATIONALISATION THE CANAL WAS TRANSFERRED TO THE RAILWAY EXECUTIVE.

1949  CANAL TRANSFERRED TO DOCKS AND INLAND WATERWAYS EXECUTIVE. (DIWE)

1950  DIWE CLOSES PARTS OF CANAL.

1951  KENNET AND AVON CANAL ASSOCIATION FORMED TO FIGHT FOR REOPENING.

1955  BRITISH TRANSPORT COMMISSION (BTC) TRIES TO GET CANAL CLOSED BY PARLIAMENT.

JOHN GOULD SUES BTC - DAMAGES SETTLED OUT OF COURT AND CANAL CLOSURE REFERRED TO PARLIAMENT.

K&ACA LAUNCHES MASSIVE CAMPAIGN TO SAVE CANAL.

1956  PARLIAMENT REFUSES TO CLOSE CANAL.

1962  CANAL TRANSFERRED TO NEW BRITISH WATERWAYS BOARD.

K&ACA BECOMES KENNET AND AVON CANAL TRUST.

1968  SCHEME AGREED FOR RESTORATION OF THE KENNET AND AVON CANAL.

K&ACT STARTS TO FINANCE RESTORATION.

Yet some serious engineering problems remained. A successful bid to the Heritage Lottery Fund by a partnership of British Waterways, The Kennet & Avon Canal Trust, The Riparian Local Authorities and The Association of Canal Enterprises (The Partnership) meant that these could be put right. Some improvements were also made towards leisure use of the canal and its environs.

Completion of that scheduled work does not remove the need to fund continued maintenance and improvement. The Partnership continues to work in harmony on many projects connected with the waterway, with education becoming more important and the Trust Museum on Devizes Wharf taking a prominent role.

# One

# Bristol to Brassknocker (Avon)

Although the Kennet & Avon Canal strictly ends at Hanham lock, just east of Bristol, it was originally conceived to link the ports of London and Bristol by an inland route. Therefore it is fitting that the images in this book should take the reader on a journey along the waterway and that such a journey should include the port of Bristol. Chapter One therefore starts at Bristol and ends at the old Avon-Wiltshire boundary in the middle of the Dundas aqueduct.

*The River Avon Navigation from Hanham to Bath was opened in 1727 and in 1796 the Kennet & Avon Canal Co. became the majority shareholder. William Jessop's floating harbour was completed in 1806, preceding the opening of the Bath to Newbury canal by four years. Until that time, vessels in the port of Bristol moored at quays along the tidal river Avon.*

Bristol was once the second most important port in the country and many canal traders found their business taking them there. Amongst them was the Midland Railway Company who had lines at Bath and Bristol and used a number of boats to provide a connection service for goods, with a canal depot at Bradford on Avon and here at Avonside Wharf Bristol. From the collection of the National Railway Museum York.

The barge Comet was originally built as a steam barge around 1890 and spent most of its life carrying grain between Bristol and Bath. It was later bought by Francis & Niblett and with the barge Dispatch continued to work the river. Francis & Niblett also carried timber from Avonmouth to Honeystreet for Robbins Lane & Pinniger until 1937. It was while owned by Francis & Niblett that the Comet, shown here c.1930, was shortened and fitted with a motor.

On Saturday 14 January 1956 a petition with 20,000 signatures against the closure of the canal left Narrow Quay Bristol and travelled by boat and canoe via Bath, Newbury, and the Thames to Westminster. Lt Cmdr C. Wray Bliss carried the petition by canoe from Bath to Churtsey Lock where it was handed over to Capt. L.R. Munk aboard the cruiser Madeleine for the rest of the journey. After being carried on a protest march to the Ministry of Transport offices in Berkeley Square it was handed to the minister, Harold Watkinson, to be forwarded to HM The Queen. Photo F. Blampied.

The barge Maria seen leaving Hanham lock. Hanham lock is the boundary between the Kennet & Avon Navigation and the Port of Bristol. Because the towing path was on the opposite side of the river to the lock the crew is having to pole the barge out of the lock and across the river to team up with the horse again. What appears to be a mast is in fact a derrick worked from the hand winch at the bow and used in the handling of cargo.

HANHAM FERRY.
Nr KEYNSHAM.

*Waiting for the ferry at Hanham lock in 1909.*

*Felix White is seen at the helm of the tar barge* Derby *in July 1955. The horizontal wheel allowed for vertical extension when the helmsman worked from a raised platform to see over loaded drums.*
Photo F. Blampied.

*Fry's confectionary factory at Keynsham Lock as it was in 1922. The large changes which can occur in water levels on the Avon is in part evidenced by the low pound in this summer scene.* From the collection of Michael E. Ware.

*The motor barge Derby is this time seen at Swineford Lock heading for Bath in July 1955. This was a daily trip to collect fifty tons of tar from Bath Gasworks. The boat would return the same day to The Bristol and West of England Tar Distillers Ltd. at Crews Hole, Bristol. Photo F. Blampied*

*The motor barge Derby in Saltford lock. This gives a good overall view of the boat, unladen and heading for Bath gasworks in June 1955. There were three tar barges on the gas works run at the time, the other two being Jolly and Isabelle. Photo F. Blampied*

*Joseph Withey established his boathouse above Kelston lock in 1896, but in 1906 he was given some competition by George Sheppard, landlord of the Jolly Sailor public house. Both businesses flourished because the long lock-free section east of Weston lock made for easy pleasure boating. At the eastern end of the 'mile reach' there were some nasty bends until 1971. It was during strong flow conditions in the 1930s that Harry Escott (see also Caroline Caen Hill (62)) was lost overboard and drowned. From the collection of Michael E. Ware.*

*Having, in 1928, aborted a proposal to apply to Parliament for the closure of the canal, GWR embarked on a substantial programme of canal maintenance. Boats were brought by rail and water from the fast declining South Wales canals to act as mud boats. In October 1929 two new steam dredgers were ordered from Stothert & Pitt of Bath. One of those dredgers, the Iron Duke is pictured here at Bath's Midland Bridge.*

*The wharves at Bath were busy long before the River Avon Navigation became part of the Kennet & Avon Canal. The River Avon already had a long history of river trade with the port of Bristol and so had a well-developed infrastructure by 1810. From the collection of Michael E. Ware*

A catastrophic failure of Widcombe Bridge occurred on 6 June 1877 resulting in the loss of ten lives. Many people had come to Bath to visit the Bath and West Show above Beechen Cliff. So many people arrived on this pedestrian toll bridge that it could not sustain the weight and it collapsed throwing everyone into the River Avon.

The canal rose from the River Avon in Bath by a flight of seven locks completed in November 1810. Today locks eight and nine have been combined as a result of road improvements into one, known as Bath Deep Lock at 18ft 8in (5.69m). Every time a boat entered or left the flight, 60,000 gallons (270,000 litres) of water were lost to the River Avon. Water shortages resulted and in 1832 the canal company acquired Thimble Mill (left in photo) at the bottom of the flight and installed a pump to pump water to the pound above lock eleven. Here a second pump returned water to the top of the flight. Attempts by the company to pump directly from the River Avon by leaving the bottom lock gates open were thwarted by the mill owners who threatened legal action unless pumping was stopped. From the collection of Wiltshire Museums Service.

*The Canal did not entirely escape the attention of Herr Hitler's Luftwaffe and in 1942 a German bomber deposited its surplus load at lock twelve, causing minimal damage.*

*Nothing remains of the upper pump-house on the Bath Flight except this ornamental chimney at Abbey View lock (lock eleven).*

*The architecture at the western end of the canal is distinctive and is characterised by the use of Bath stone. The style of this lock cottage at Bath top lock seen here c.1950 can be seen repeated as far east as Seend. This lock cottage has had close associations with at least two generations of the Mizen family, originally from South Wraxall near Bradford-on-Avon. In a census of 1891 David Mizen, youngest son of Robert, was the lock keeper here. His eldest brother, Emanuel, was listed as a canal labourer in 1891 and Robert, the father, lived here in the later stages of his life.*

*This pair of narrow boats belonging to the Gerrish family is seen approaching Bath top lock c.1890. The wharf on the left opposite the horse is the Somerset Coal Canal Wharf, beyond which at right angles to the lock can be seen the stable block. The Gerrish family became well known for challenging GWR over delays and overcharging, with frequent success.*

This early photograph, c.1860, depicts the fast Scotch boats, apparently by this time unused, moored near the top of the Bath Flight of locks alongside the Bairds Maltings Wharf. The 'Scotch' boat was first tested and put into service between Bath and Bradford on Avon in 1833 having been leased by the canal company to Richard Parker who operated from nearby Sydney Wharf.

Trials had shown no bank-wash at a speed of 8 to 9mph (13 to 14kph). The boat provided first and second class accommodation for the one and a half hour journey, twice a day excluding Sundays. In 1840 the business was taken over by Packer and Kinver. Then in 1852 the canal was taken over by GWR who, by 1854 had imposed a 4mph (6kph) speed limit; this service seems to have ceased soon after this date.

The ghostly form of a boat on the far right has been interpreted by some that have studied this image as being a Severn Trow. A number of these craft were owned by the canal company to facilitate direct trading to and from the River Severn and some were produced by Robbins Lane & Pinniger at Honeystreet. However, the proximity of this craft to the Somerset Coal Canal wharf could equally mean that it is a Kennet barge with the derrick raised. (see the photo of the barge Maria leaving Hanham Lock).

Leaving Sydney Wharf in an easterly direction the canal passes through a tunnel under Cleveland House, following which it emerges into the splendour of Sydney Gardens. The canal company acquired the property in the 1920s, which must have been very soon after it was built, for their headquarters. It was vacated by GWR, the new canal owners, in 1864 and all surviving records were moved to Paddington. A small rectangular hole can still be seen in the tunnel roof and the story is told that messages were passed through it from the headquarters above to passing boatmen. Consideration of the practicalities of such an arrangement leads one to assume a more mundane function for the shaft.

As restoration of the canal commenced, there was a natural eagerness to use the stretches that emerged in water for navigation. The most suitable craft at the time were paddle boats. Several of these have made their mark in history: one is seen here at Bath and was used as a trip boat in the Bath/Bathampton area.

Emerging from the Cleveland House tunnel the canal enters Sydney Gardens and looking over one's shoulder, this splendid view is revealed. Sydney Gardens was a private venture and in 1798 the canal company had to pay a fee of 2,000 guineas for authority to route this waterway through the gardens. The ornate iron footbridges were chosen by the Sydney Gardens Proprietors from the Coalbrookdale Company and erected in 1800.

*This scene sees boys of the Percy Boys'
Club, Bath clearing rubbish from the canal
in Sydney Gardens in 1964 during the
restoration period. Photo by F. Blampied.*

*The canal now leaves Sydney Gardens by a short tunnel. Above the portal as one leaves the gardens is
a stone tablet depicting the face of a bearded man. It is claimed that this ornamental carving depicts
Father Thames and a similar female face on the portal of Cleveland House tunnel represents Sabrina
or the River Severn. It sounds reasonable, though no supporting documentary evidence has been found.*

Hy. Crouch
Lock Keeper
Foxhangers
Devizes

Great Western Railway.
Kennet and Avon Canal.
Engineer's Office.
Devizes, August 15th 1894

Lately it has been found that Lock Keepers have in distinct Violation of the Company's regulations permitted Rowing Boats & other Pleasure Boats to ply on the Canal and pass the Locks on a Sunday I therefore in writing repeat the regulation which every Lock Keeper have already been made aware of, namely that unless specially authorised no Traffic is to be allowed on the Canal during any Sunday. Therefore if any Boats attempts to navigate the Canal on a Sunday the Lock Keeper must demand (Respectfully) the production of the Permit point out the conditions on which it is issued and stop the Boat untill Monday Morning no Boat to be allowed to pass through or be carried over any Locks, if the occupants of a Boat after the observance of the above refuse to obey the conditions of the Permit their names and addresses must be demanded and if refused the Boat must be followed untill they are obtained and the Violation of rule must, with the names &C be reported to me at once. Any omission to carry out these instructions will be treated as a neglect of duty and a fine will be imposed in accordance with the degree of neglect This notice must be pasted up and kept for future reference.

C. J. Hart
per T. Harding

One of the rules of the Canal Company, and subsequently GWR, prevented trading on a Sunday. It is reputed that a chain was hung across Sydney Gardens tunnel to enforce this rule, but clearly the rule was occasionally broken. This letter from GWR Engineer's Office in Devizes to lockkeepers details the steps to be taken to enforce the rule and the penalties for failure in this respect.

*Just east of Sydney Garden Tunnel was Darlington Wharf. It was from here that the Scotch boats departed for the passenger service to Bradford-on-Avon. It is assumed that the passengers used the towpath side of the canal, as the wharf on the offside was used until the 1870s by a coal merchant and a boat builder. In 1869 the area became a public bathing place.*

*William Harbutt's plasticine factory on the left no longer exists. Harbutt built his factory on the site of Harbutt's Mill and during building of the canal the route had to swing to fit between the mill and the George Inn on the right. Harbutt's factory received deliveries of coke by canal.*

# DAILY CONVEYANCE

BY THE

## KENNET & AVON CANAL,

AND

## *Great Western Railway,*

TO AND FROM

## *LONDON,*

## BATH & BRISTOL,

### And all parts of the West of England, Ireland, &c.

## PARKER, RANDELL, & Co.

Respectfully inform their Friends and the Public that on TUESDAY, the 8th of December next, they will commence as Carriers, with their new fast Iron Boats, in connexion with the Rail, for the conveyance of all description of Goods and Passengers to and from the above places, at reduced rates.

Having made arrangements with the Kennet and Avon Canal and the Great Western Railway Companies, they are enabled to convey Goods from

### London to Bath & Bristol in ONE CLEAR DAY.

The Public may be assured of strict attention being paid to their favors.

Goods in quantities not less than half a ton, will be fetched from any part of the City or London Docks, free of any additional charge, on notice being forwarded to Messrs. DEACON & Co. Cripplegate; and all Goods intended for this Conveyance must be at Cripplegate before Four o'clock P.M.

### Please to order per Parker, Randell, & Co. as under:

| | | |
|---|---|---|
| LONDON | Deacon & Co. | *White Horse, Cripplegate.* |
| READING | J. S Randell | *Reading Wharf.* |
| NEWBURY | John Adey | *West Mills Wharf.* |
| HUNGERFORD | — Neel, Jun. | *Hungerford Wharf.* |
| MARLBOROUGH | Jeremiah Hammond | *Office, High Street.* |
| DEVIZES | Daniel Phipps | *Devizes Wharf.* |
| TROWBRIDGE | | |
| FROME | | |
| WARMINSTER | Walter Newth | *Hilperton Wharf.* |
| WESTBURY | | |
| BRADFORD | J. Sainsbury | *Barge Inn.* |
| BATH | Rd. Parker | *Office, Christopher Inn, Market Place.* |
| BRISTOL | —Stephens | *Three Queens, Thomas Street.* |

**NOTICE.**—All Goods which shall be delivered for the purpose of being carried, will be considered as GENERAL LIENS, and subject not only for the Money due for the Carriage of such particular Goods, but also to the general balance due from their respective Owner or Owners to the Proprietors of the said Conveyances.

Goods suffered to remain in any of their Warehouses more than Twenty-four Hours after their Arrival, will be at the sole risk of the respective Owners thereof.

The Proprietors will not be responsible for Writings, Paintings, China, Glass, Liquors in Bottles, Furniture, Furs, or Carriages, under any circumstances whatever: nor for Money, Plate, Jewels, Rings, Watches, Silk, or Lace, unless entered as such, and Insurance be paid besides the common rate of Carriage, when delivered to their care: neither will they pay above £10 for loss or damage of any Package, unless the same shall have been entered as of a higher value, and an Insurance paid thereon in the way above specified.

All Goods packed in a damp or improper state, or in returned packages, or sent with inaccurate addresses, will be at the Owners' risk.

Persons sending Aqua-fortis, Oil of Vitriol, or other Ardent Spirits, or dangerous articles, will be held accountable for any damage arising therefrom, unless the contents are truly described on the direction, so that due care may be taken by the Proprietors in loading them.

Any Goods or Packages that shall have remained Three Months in the Warehouse without being claimed, or on account of the non-payment of the charges will be sold to defray the Carriage and other charges thereon, or the general lien, as the case may be, with Warehouse Rent and Expenses.

## DEACON & Co. Agents,

### WHITE HORSE INN, CRIPPLEGATE, LONDON.

*The service offered by Parker Randell & Co. used a combination of fast iron Scotch boats and the Great Western Railway line. The service was for passengers and goods but this poster does not indicate where the canal/railway interchange took place.*

*This delightful autumn scene was captured at Bathampton road bridge c.1950. Travelling east it was the last road bridge over the canal before arriving at Hampton Quarry Wharf at the foot of Bathampton Down. The bridge carried traffic on a link between two major roads while the canal below was once busy with boats carrying stone from the quarries on Bathampton Down and which had been loaded at Hampton Quarry Wharf.*

*In 1926 GWR announced an intention to apply to Parliament for closure of the canal. Such was the public protes, that by 1928 the idea had been abandoned. Robbins Lane & Pinniger were constantly harassing GWR, with success, over the state of the canal. In 1929 GWR ordered two new luffing jib steam dredgers from Stothert & Pitt of Bath to add to the grab dredgers already in use. This picture was taken near Bathampton in the late 1930s.*

*The pound between Bath top lock and Bradford-on-Avon lock is nine miles of beautiful, lock free navigation. Therefore it has always been popular with trip boats such as the* Maroherita, *seen here c.1920 near Bathampton. From the collection of Michael E. Ware.*

*GWR did not allow the use of steam powered boats on the canal except by special permission. It was claimed that their speed caused bank wash, necessitating more frequent dredging. So this narrow boat in the Bath Valley is horse drawn; the picture is one of the few such photographs of the Kennet & Avon surviving. From the collection of Michael E. Ware*

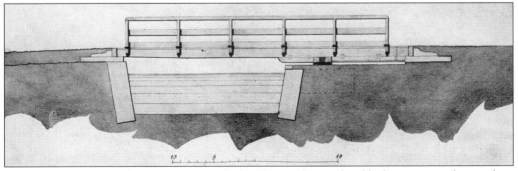

*Leaving Bathampton and continuing towards the Thames the canal suddenly swings south as it skirts Bathampton Down. Almost immediately there is Bathampton swing-bridge, the first of many such bridges before Reading. Like all the canal architecture, they were designed by John Rennie. This is one of his original drawings of c.1794.*

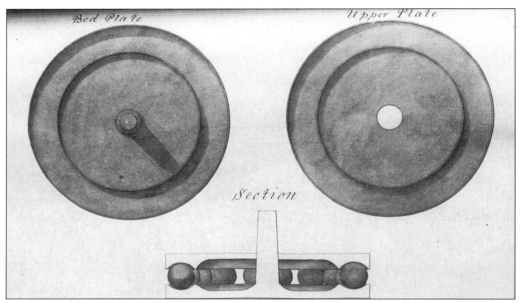

*Bed Plate*       *Upper Plate*

*Section*

It is said that John Rennie was the first civil engineer to use the ball race to facilitate easier opening of swing-bridges. This may well be true but this drawing of his fails to convey the mass of such castings. The race is held together only by the weight of the bridge which needs to be perfectly balanced. Such a ball race can be seen in the canal museum on Devizes Wharf or under those swing-bridges still in use.

As trade diminished the canal slipped into disuse and many boats were abandoned. This one is pictured near Bathampton c.1935. Photo by J.E. Manners.

*Claverton pumping station supplies water from the River Avon to the western end of the canal. This pump-house was erected on the site of Claverton Mill to house the pump, driven by a water wheel. The building was completed in October 1810 and the pump was working early in 1813. The machinery was made in John Rennie's London workshop.*

*The water wheel of Claverton pump is impressive. It is over 17ft (5m) in diameter and 24ft (7m) wide, breast shot from the mill pond.* Photo by Philip Wilson.

*Midland Railway Co.'s boat No.3 leaves Brassknocker Basin heading for Bath. With depots at Bristol and Bath it seemed a good idea to use the canal as a feeder service to those depots. It was never very successful and the service appears to have ceased c.1900. This photograph suggests a passenger service, of sorts, as well as a goods service.*

*Although the GWR did not encourage pleasure boating, the scenery through the Bath Valley proved to be a strong magnet as shown by this party thought to be in celebration of Queen Victoria's diamond jubilee in 1897.*

*The excursion continues and it becomes even more evident that it is marking an important event.*

*It seems that a violin and a harp were used to provide a musical accompaniment to the party. The Union Jacks and the pith helmet of the helmsman further suggest a national celebration as the party breaks at Brassknocker Wharf.*

To maintain a lock-free nine mile pound from Bath to Bradford-on-Avon the canal crossed the Avon valley twice. This aqueduct at Brassknocker was designed by Rennie in Doric style with three spans beneath its length of 150ft (46m). Named after Charles Dundas, chairman of the canal company, it is an architectural delight in local Bath stone.

On various structures of Bath stone along the canal can be found a wide variety of marks chiseled into the masonry. This one is photographed on the trough of the Dundas Aqueduct, and they are known collectively as Masons' Marks. Such embellishment was the mason's individual way of marking the construction work he had accomplished so that it could be assessed and he could be paid accordingly.

This view shows Dundas Aqueduct c.1930 across the top of the crane at Brassknocker Wharf from the A36 road to Bath.

The canal to the left heads for Bath and to the right, just out of view, is the entrance to the Somerset Coal Canal. Across the aqueduct the canal turns sharp right (south) towards Avoncliffe. A dark line in the trees on the side of the hill opposite, is the remains of the tramroad leading down from Conkwell stone quarry. The tram road terminated at a wharf to the left of the canal just before the right turn. The quarry opened in 1801 to supply building stone for the canal but was found to be of poor quality. The tow path is on the right of the canal.

This view of the entrance to the Somerset Coal Canal was captured from Dundas Bridge c.1900. For most of the nineteenth century this was a busy junction. The entrance is marked by the closed lock gates and the stone bridge, neither feature existing today. The towpath crosses Dundas Bridge, then passes along the wharf, over the stone bridge and along the aqueduct. The flanged iron post, just behind the central cow, prevented the tow-line cutting across the corner. The stone pillars in the foreground support a wooden roller on a steel axle to which a windlass could be attached. The roller would have been attached to a chain connected to a wooden plug, fitting stone cappings, over a drain in the bed of the canal. With the attendant closure of appropriate stop gates the plug could literally be pulled on a section of canal to drain it for maintenance.

The toll collector's hut, a most important if small building, is just out of shot under the bank behind the corner of the warehouse. It still exists, for those interested in visiting this interesting and unspoiled piece of the canal. From the collection of D.L. McDougall.

On 1 July 1984, Dundas aqueduct was reopened to navigation after lengthy restoration. The event was permanently commemorated by the unveiling of a plaque on the wharf, the honours being performed by General Stockwell, president of the Kennet & Avon Canal Trust. Admiral Sir William O'Brien (chairman of the trust) here applauds at the moment of unveiling. Photo by Tony Wadley

This is the lock cottage of the Somerset Coal Canal c.1900, the gable end of which can just be seen in the trees to the right in the previous photograph of the canal. It should be noted that the lock is narrow as opposed to the broad locks of the Kennet & Avon Canal.

# SOMERSET COAL CANAL LOCKS.

## Trader's Permit, No. 16

| No. of Boat. | Cargo. | From whence |
|---|---|---|
| 1 | Coal | Paulton |

| Owner's Name. | Steerer's Name. |
|---|---|
| Freegard | Geo |

| No. of Tons. | | Lockage. | | |
|---|---|---|---|---|
| | | £ | s. | d. |
| 28 | At One Shilling per Ton ...... | 1 | 8 | |

Canal Office, Midford,

May 22 1860

*W. Tuckwell*    Toll Clerk.

---

*The Somerset coalfields provided a considerable amount of trade along the Kennet & Avon Canal via the coal canal. The Somerset Coal Canal was completed in 1805 and went into liquidation in 1893 although pumping to the summit continued until 1903. The demise of this important arm was brought about by the arrival of the railway at the collieries in 1874 and the gradual closure of most of the pits. This toll ticket for the coal canal was issued at Midford on 22 May 1860. The charge was £1 8s 0d (£1.40) for 28 tons. A further toll would have been payable at Brassknocker or Bradford-on-Avon for transit along the Kennet & Avon Canal.*

*These grooves are seen in the iron post referred to previously on the inside of the approach bend to the Dundas Aqueduct. It is a good illustration of how the gritty tow ropes of the horse drawn boats were capable of cutting into iron and why iron protection is often still to be seen on some masonry features along the canal.*

*This view of Brassknocker Basin and Dundas Bridge was taken c.1959, prior to restoration, looking from the entrance to the coal canal. The derelict wide boat, too big for the coal canal, adds to the general sense of desolation at this time.*

# Two

# Brassknocker Wharf to Froxfield Wharf (Wiltshire)

At the mid-point of the Dundas Aqueduct, travelling east, one enters the County of Wiltshire, which the canal proceeds to cut across the middle. The architecture of the structures associated with the canal gradually changes as the journey progresses, influenced in part by a gradual distancing from the Bath stone quarries.

*Contrary to popular belief, GWR was not responsible for neglect of the canal to the point where closure was necessary. The GWR Act No.1 of 1852 and the Regulation of Railways Act, section 17, of 1873 placed clear maintenance responsibilities upon the Railway Co. as the owners of the canal. GWR accepted these responsibilities and acted accordingly, though sometimes it needing pushing. The canal was maintained in a (just) navigable condition, right up to nationalisation in January 1948. This photograph, taken on 8 August 1917 between Dundas and Avoncliffe aqueducts, shows a canal drained for just such bank maintenance.*

*Bank and bed leaks being repaired near Limpley Stoke during a stoppage in April 1921.*

*Complaints against the Great Western Railway by the boatmen frequently concerned the need for dredging. This spoon dredger is under tow near Limpley Stoke c.1920, possibly in preparation for work at a new location.*

The Kennet barge was an impressive boat at 69ft (21m) long, 13ft 19in (4.2m) beam and a laden draft of 4ft (1.2m). This one is the Pearl in 1892, approaching Limpley Stoke Bridge, heading for Bristol riding high in the water and clearly unladen. Robbins Lane & Pinniger built a number of these craft for United Alkali of Bristol, all of which were named after precious stones. This must have been a very special journey, as the gentleman leaning against the winch sports business attire and a bowler hat. The helmsman is similarly well dressed and with the boat riding so high it is possible that the Pearl is being delivered to United Alkali.

The canal between Dundas Aqueduct and Bradford-on-Avon was called 'The Dry Section' due to the regular leaks that developed, requiring sections to be drained for repair. The cause was underlying fissured limestone channeling water and thus causing slippage, subsidence, leaks and even bursts of the waterway. In 1966/67 as part of the canal restoration, trials were carried out with heavy-duty polythene sheeting protected by a layer of concrete as seen here at Murhill Quarry Wharf. Although successful at sealing the canal bed, these early trials were stopped in order that attention might be focussed on other more pressing matters. The raised section of the wharf was the plinth for the wharf crane.

*Pleasure use of the canal, except by special permission, was not encouraged. Yet here c.1900 the beauty of the valley at Murhill Quarry Wharf was not to be resisted by this couple. In the middle distance is a narrowing of the canal with two sets of opposing stop gates which could be closed to isolate sections of canal for draining and maintenance. In theory, in the event of a sudden and disastrous breach the rush of water would automatically close such gates. They were most commonly to be found between Dundas Aqueduct and Bradford-on-Avon where leaks frequent.*

*The boundaries of the property of the Kennet & Avon Canal Co. were marked by stones, similar to milestones, but marked simply 'KA'. The Great Western Railway Co. took over the Canal in 1852 and subsequently markers were produced in cast iron. This one was revealed at Murhill during clearance work in the mid-1960s and is a typical example. Measuring approximately 7in (18cm) in diameter and 2in (5cm) thick of solid cast iron, they were frequently cast onto the end of a length of GWR rail which was driven into the ground. Hence many can still be found today.*

Not many images of boats under tow on the Kennet & Avon Canal seem to have survived and even fewer which suggest the enjoyment of home comforts in the cabin by either a boatman or a boat family. But this boat, seen clothed up and rounding the bend at Limpley Stoke, has a good fire going in the cabin. There appear to be two horses on the towpath side by side which suggests that two boats might be about to pass in opposite directions.

In the early days of restoration of the canal, attempts were made to stop leaks in the length from Dundas Aqueduct to Bradford-on-Avon using clay puddle. Taken on 3 October 1965 the photograph shows clay being loaded at Limpley Stoke Bridge onto the wagons of a tramway laid on the canal bed. The attempts were unsuccessful and the work was halted in 1966. Photo F. Blampied.

*A workboat and maintenance gang work their way from Winsley Bridge towards Avoncliffe in the early 1920s.*

*The Kennet & Avon Canal has always attracted walkers in the Bath to Bradford-on-Avon area. This is certainly no young couple taking a stroll near Winsley c.1905.*

At Avoncliffe the canal again crosses the River Avon and the railway. Avoncliffe aqueduct is not as ornate as the Dundas aqueduct but is longer and a sag in the middle is most noticeable at the parapet. This was the view c.1900 looking to the south-east. Beyond the aqueduct Randell, Saunders & Co. had a stone quarry at Westwood. A tramway led to the wharf on the far side, with a rail extension along the towpath, which can be seen in the foreground to descend to a railway siding.

During the First World War the old workhouse at Avoncliffe was requisitioned as a Red Cross convalescent hospital for soldiers, who were sent there from Bath Hospital. Mrs Fletcher from Bradford-on-Avon arranged the acquisition of the barge Bittern as a means of transporting men to and from the public house beside the road bridge at Bradford. It was a regular afternoon trip with Mrs Fletcher at the helm. The horse was stabled near the Old Tavern Inn at Bradford and the trips continued throughout the summer months of 1917 and 1918.

*Like the iron post on the Dundas Aqueduct this stone stands on the south-east corner of Avoncliffe Aqueduct and bears the scars of over 100 years of guiding gritty tow ropes as the horse takes up the tow around the bend.*

The trip boat Maroherita pulls into Lower Wharf at Bradford-on-Avon c.1920 with a load of well-dressed boys, possibly a school trip. This boat ran regularly between Bath and Bradford and is probably using Lower Wharf as a drop point for the crew who will work the lock. The lock is immediately beyond the road bridge and the lower gates can be seen to be open. Leaving lower gates open was a standard requirement on much of the canal owing to the lack of bypass weirs. Bradford-on-Avon Wharf lies immediately beyond the lock. Lower Wharf dealt mostly with local trade, coal in particular.

Bradford-on-Avon was an important town on the canal in the nineteenth century but, by the time that this picture was taken in about 1920, trade at the wharf was in serious decline. In the centre of the middle ground can be seen the gauging dock with the quarter ton stones and crane on the left. A company agent and toll collector were stationed at this wharf, which was owned first by the canal company and then, after 1852, by the Great Western Railway Co. The two boats moored on the right are immediately above the top gates of the lock and would be making passage through the lock difficult for any other craft.

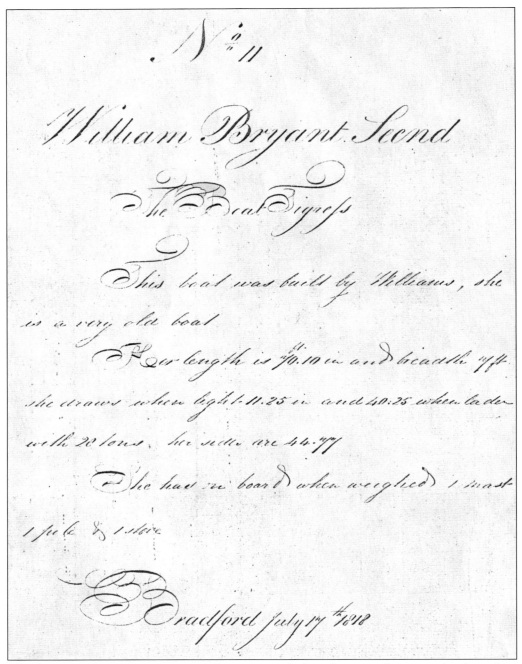

William Bryant Seend

The Boat Tigress

This boat was built by Williams, she is a very old boat

Her length is 70. 10 in and breadth 7ft. she draws when light 11.25 in and 40.25 when laden with 20 tons, her sides are 44.77

She had on board when weighed 1 mast 1 pole & 1 store

Bradford July 17th 1818

*This document, from 1818, was extremely important. It shows how records were made when a boat was gauged. All boats had to be gauged. This record shows that gauging was carried out on July 17 1818 for the boat Tigress owned by William Bryant of Seend and the description states that it was built by Williams and was already an old boat. The stated dimensions make it a narrow boat, 70ft 10in in length, and draught dimensions are given at a loading of 28 tons.*

## William Bryant. Seend
### The Boat Tigress

| Tons. | Dry Inches. | Difference. | Unloading. | Tons. | Dry Inches. | Difference. | Unloading. | Tons. | Dry Inches. | Difference. | Unloading. |
|---|---|---|---|---|---|---|---|---|---|---|---|
| 0 | 33.52 | | | | | | | | | | |
| 1 | 32.44 | 1.08 | | | | | | | | | |
| 2 | 31.36 | | | | | | | | | | |
| 3 | 30.28 | | | | | | | | | | |
| 4 | 29.20 | | | | | | | | | | |
| 5 | 28.15 | | | | | | | | 35.15 | 1.63 | | |
| 6 | 27.10 | | | | | | | | | | |
| 7 | 26.05 | | | | | | | | | | |
| 8 | 25.00 | | | | | | | | | | |
| 9 | 23.96 | | | | | | | | | | |
| 10 | 22.92 | | | | | | | | | | |
| 11 | 21.88 | | | | | | | | | | |
| 12 | 20.84 | | | | | | | | | | |
| 13 | 19.80 | | | | | | | | | | |
| 14 | 18.76 | | | | | | | | | | |
| 15 | 17.72 | | | | | | | | | | |
| 16 | 16.68 | | | | | | | | | | |
| 17 | 15.65 | | | | | | | | | | |
| 18 | 14.62 | | | | | | | | | | |
| 19 | 13.59 | | | | | | | | | | |
| 20 | 12.56 | | | | | | | | | | |
| 21 | 11.55 | | | | | | | | | | |
| 22 | 10.54 | | | | | | | | | | |
| 23 | 9.53 | | | | | | | | | | |
| 24 | 8.52 | | | | | | | | | | |
| 25 | 7.52 | | | | | | | | | | |
| 26 | 6.52 | | | | | | | | | | |
| 27 | 5.53 | | | | | | | | | | |
| 28 | 4.52 | | | | | | | | | | |
| 29 | 3.52 | | | | | | | | | | |
| 30 | 2.52 | | | | | | | | | | |

The purpose of gauging was to allow measurement of the height of the gunwale above the water line (the dry inches) for known loads. Thus a toll collector could measure the dry inches of any boat to determine the weight of cargo being carried and charge a toll, in accordance with the class of goods, at so many pence per ton per mile. The dry inches were measured with a calibrated gauging staff and there is one exhibited in the Canal Museum on Devizes wharf. During boat gauging the dry inches were measured at four fixed plates, two on each side of the boat, and averaged. Using the stone blocks and a crane, as in the photograph at the bottom of page 51, the weight in the boat was gradually increased and a record of dry inches made at regular intervals. The gauging record up to 30 tons is entered on the left and subsequent entries in the top right hand corner record the unladen freeboard from 1835 to 1840. This record would have been laboriously hand copied and supplied to all toll collection points where the boat was likely to trade.

*This view shows Bradford-on-Avon lock cottage beside the lock, c.1920. The figures are those of the lock-keeper and his wife.*

*The excursion party last encountered at Brassknocker Wharf is caught here at Bradford-on-Avon. We can recognise the same members of the party but the pith helmet of the helmsman seems to be missing. The mass display of Union Jacks adds weight to the belief that this is a special trip in celebration of Queen Victoria's diamond jubilee in July 1897. The very observant might even note that the boat is splendidly painted and clean in comparison with those work-boats lined with canvas covers for Sunday School outings and shown elsewhere in the book.*

*The British Waterways Board house on the wharf-side at Bradford-on-Avon, photographed here in the 1920s, still exists today but as a private house.*

*This large outing is of the local Friendly Society at Hilperton Wharf near Trowbridge in the 1870s. In 1877 GWR charged £2 for a canoe on the canal, a large sum at that time and further evidence of its policy of discouraging pleasure craft.*

Both of the locks at Semington can be seen in this photograph taken from the road bridge c.1920. It is also possible to see the entrance to the Wilts and Berks Canal, known to the Moira boatmen as the Ippey Cut; the Kennet & Avon was known as the Kensit. From 1810 to about 1876 this was a busy junction. In 1860, 40,861 tons of coal were carried from Semington onto the Wilts and Berks.

| PERMIT the Boat Nº 1 Owner Geo Keelard | | | | | | |
|---|---|---|---|---|---|---|
| Steered by Jno Teagle to pass on the WILTS AND BERKS CANAL, | | | | | | |
| Loaded as under, at the risk and peril of the said Owner. | | | | | | |
| LOADED AT. | BOUND TO. | CARGO. | WEIGHT TONS. | NO. OF MILES. | RATE. | AMOUNT. £ s. d. |
| Semington | Dauntsey | Coals | 2 82 | 15 | 1ᵈ | 1 15 9½ |
| COMPANY'S NUMBER. 1197. | DATE 1860 20ᵗʰ August | Granted at Semington Paid at Payable at Dº | | | £ John Theobald Toll Collector. | |

A toll ticket issued at Semington in 1860. Semington Wharf was owned by the Kennet & Avon Canal Co. and was situated on the south side of the canal between the road bridge and Biss Aqueduct.

The lock cottage beside Semington bottom lock. Between 1939 and 1945 the lock-keeper at Semington was a Mr Buckley and lock fifteen became known as 'Buckley's Lock'. Mr Buckley can be seen standing in the middle of the punt; on the far left is six-year-old Bill Read with his younger brother. Young Bill Read successfully fished the canal with a fishing rod made for him by Mr Buckley. The Read family had moved to Semington c.1941 as Bill's Father was in the RAF and posted to Melksham in that year. The family was shown great kindness by Mr and Mrs Buckley and in 1942 they allowed the Reads to live in the lock cottage with them.

Mr H.W. Anderson gave testimony as to the state of the canal in 1912 in an account of a journey from Byfleet on the River Wey to Bath. The purpose of the journey was to visit a newly married family friend, Mrs Hardy (nee Boothby), in fulfillment of an earlier promise. The journey was by skiff, with a group of friends leaving Twickenham in a second skiff, the two parties meeting at Shepperton for the rest of the journey. In this photograph the parties are seen at Semington lock. Left to right: from Byfleet – Mr Anderson, lock keeper, Mrs Hardy, lock children, Mr Brown; from Twickenham – Mr Faulkender, Mrs Shoreland, Mr Shoreland.

Mr Anderson in his account of the journey used words often repeated in more recent times.

Working the locks and bridges ourselves caused great delay and they are mostly in indifferent order and very stiff and we had to land at each for this purpose, so a lot of time was lost especially as the lock had to be emptied after us when we were ascending, or we had to wait for it to be filled before use in descending causing extreme delay again. One wants to be strong and fit to do this sort of work rapidly and it took more 'beef' and perspiration out of you than hours of rowing did... Many gates were difficult to open owing to the great leakage through the other pair of gates and sluices had to be left fully open before the gates would move... We met but little traffic between Reading and Bath and we were looked on as curios...

Despite the physical exertions the party found the 310 mile round journey '... a most enjoyable one...'. They were apparently captivated by the towns, the foliage and the flowers. Photos by H.W. Anderson with album loaned to K&A Trust by Mr M.W. Anderson 1987.

In 1967 Capt. John Mansfield Robinson CBE RN started the Junior Division of the Kennet & Avon Canal Trust and harnessed the energy of youth to help in restoration of the canal. Capt. Mansfield Robinson was most innovative and developed the weed cutter *Moonraker*, which was a familiar sight on the canal during restoration years.

*A view of Seend top lock c.1910 with Rusty Lane swing-bridge just visible in the background.*

*Between locks nineteen and twenty in the Seend flight of five locks was the nineteenth-century iron works on the south side of the canal. The site was first exploited by J.E. Holloway in 1856 and had a short turbulent period of success peaking from 1873 to 1888 under Richard Burridge. The rails in the bottom left hand corner lead down to Seend Wharf opposite the Barge Inn. From the collection of Wiltshire County Council/Seend Women's Institute*

*The twenty-nine locks up to Devizes are traversed by a number of road bridges, each with a separate towpath tunnel, as this one at Marsh Lane. The Devizes flight was the last section of canal to be completed in 1810. The two halves of the canal were connected by a tramway, hence the tunnels.*

*The house on the right of the previous picture is now viewed from a different aspect. Originally owned by the Kennet & Avon Canal Co., it was once occupied by John Blackwell, one of the company's engineers. This photograph was taken in 1884, thirty-two years after the Great Western Railway Co. took over the canal. The elderly gentleman seated on the left is Mr Balding of GWR.*

*Above Marsh Lane lock lies Mash Lane Basin and wharves, followed by the dramatic flight of Caen Hill's sixteen locks each with side ponds. This view dates from c.1910.*

*The boats Caroline and Apollo wait for the lock to fill as they ascend Caen Hill c.1870. Caroline was owned by H. Escott and registered at Seend.*

*A rural scene here at Caen Hill. Frederick Fielding, 'cowkeeper' for a local farm sits on the beam of the top gates of lock thirty-eight while his son Walter, born 1884, carries milk to Springfield House where the family lived. It still stands today.*

*By 1955 Caen Hill presented a sorry, derelict sight. The first clearance of debris, mud and bushes from the flight was carried out by the trust's Junior Division volunteers.*

*Lock forty-two on the Caen Hill flight being cleared by young volunteers in 1972.*

*The canal was reopened to navigation by Her Majesty the Queen in August 1990 at lock forty-four. However, this was not to be the end of the restoration story. Serious engineering problems remained, which were only solved with the help of Heritage Lottery Funding.*

*Caen Hill top lock (forty-four) and lock cottage c.1910. It has changed little today and is now a tearoom.*

*Devizes, like Bath, utilised part of the canal as a swimming pool. Lock forty-eight is in the background beyond the swimming pool as soldiers of the Transport Division undergo boat handling*

*training in preparation for operations in Europe in the First World War.* Photograph courtesy of The Imperial War Museum London.

*Engineers of the Inland Water Transport Section established a special boat handling school in Devizes during the First World War. As the Bedford and the Essex enter lock fifty to descend the Devizes flight, the notice advertising pleasure boats seems a little out of place.* Photograph courtesy of the Imperial War Museum, London.

*Lock fifty is the top lock of the Devizes flight of locks and marks the beginning of fifteen miles of lock-free canal through Pewsey Vale to Wootton Rivers. Where the towpath descends through the old tramway tunnel, deep grooves can be seen to have been cut by tow ropes in the iron plate protecting the masonry and in the masonry of the arch as boats were hauled into the lock.*

*William Dickenson's wide boat Croxley loads grain at Devizes Town Wharf c.1900.*

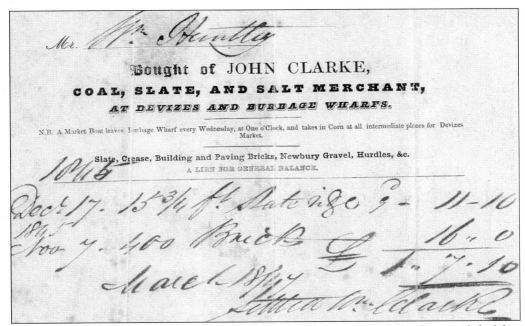

*John Clarke traded on Devizes Wharf and it would appear that customers had to be reminded of their debts. This bill for fifteen ridge slates and 400 bricks was settled in March 1847, but the goods were bought between November and December 1845.*

*Robbins Lane and Pinniger barge* Unity *is moored at Lower Wharf Devizes between lock fifty and Town Wharf. It is loaded with empty acid carboys being returned from the fertilizer plant at Honeystreet to Avonmouth c.1910. The late Tom Hams, last captain of* Unity, *related how it took two horses to haul the barge up the River Avon from Bristol but only one to return the empties. Two*

*days after the empty barge set off on the return trip from Honeystreet, the second horse would be put on the train at Woodborough to meet up with the boat at Bristol. If room permitted, one horse could instead be tethered on the boat. GWR considered the acid cargo to be too dangerous to consign to rail transport. The small building in the middle ground is the stable block.*

Sixty years after seeing William Dickenson at work, the scene has changed to one of decay. Today however the wharf is again a thriving area benefiting this time from leisure. The building beside the canal is now a theatre.

During the prosperous years of the canal six wharves were in use within the borders of Devizes, though only Town Wharf was a toll collection point. Today just the town wharf survives. The long low building with the verandah was a grain warehouse, then later a bonded warehouse.

*Two more of William Dickenson's boats, the* Ceres *and the* Faith, *decked out for what appears to be a Sunday school outing from Devizes c.1900. Note the common form of hat design worn by some of the ladies.* From the collection of F. Blampied.

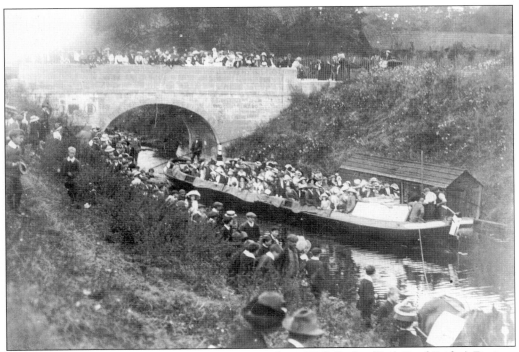

*This Sunday school outing is captured c.1900 at Quakers' Walk Bridge (Park Road Bridge) Devizes.*

73

*Devizes fire brigade is seen here utilising the canal to carry out a pump test at Cemetery Road Bridge Devizes during the Second World War. Of particular interest are the anti-tank emplacements (Dragons' Teeth) constructed at a time when the Kennet & Avon formed part of a National defence line. Note also the hooded headlamps and respirators hung round the spotlight.*

*A GWR working flat, a typical work-boat c.1910, pictured at Devizes between Quakers' Walk and London Road.*

The annual canoe race was born in 1948 when a £20 prize was offered by a group of people from Devizes to any Devizes scout group that could navigate a boat from Devizes to Westminster in under 100 hours. Four scouts were successful with two old canoes, and the following year it became an annual event. It is now an international canoe race, held every Easter, with several competition categories.

This Sunday school outing is pictured on the south side of Townsend Bridge, Horton, c.1918. The hazy gable end of the lengthsman's cottage can be seen behind the boat. This was to become the home of the late General Stockwell, a former chairman of the Kennet & Avon Canal Trust.

*A much less happy scene taken from almost the same position as the previous picture, c.1945, approximately twenty-seven years later. Photo by F. Merritt.*

*The Charlotte Dundas was an early Kennet & Avon Canal trip boat, built from an old dredger pontoon recovered during restoration of the canal and fitted with a 30hp diesel engine and hydraulically powered paddles. Only paddles could cope with the weed encountered in the early stages of restoration. The Charlotte Dundas is seen here at Honeystreet c.1975.*

The original Barge Inn at Honeystreet was built in 1810 but was destroyed by fire in 1858. It was an important midway provisioning point on the canal, possessing a bakery, a slaughterhouse, a brewery and stocking general provisions. It was thus rebuilt within six months. The lantern roof seen here in 1895 no longer exists.

*During the Second World War, the canal through Wiltshire and Berkshire was part of a defensive line in case of invasion. Along with the anti-tank 'Dragons' Teeth' on all the bridges were the brick and concrete 'Pill Boxes'. These were to be manned and armed with rifles, machine guns or anti tank weapons depending on design and position. This example was photographed at Honeystreet in 1994.*

*A few of these 'Pill Boxes' were disguised like this one, also at Honeystreet.*

*Honeystreet was the base of Robbins Lane & Pinniger (formerly Robbins & Co.) who had a boat building business on the north bank of the canal and a timber yard on the south (towpath) bank. Pictured c.1910 the barge is moored in front of the boat building shed.*

Honey Street Wharf (2)  Woodborough

*A more general photograph of Honeystreet Wharf c.1895 shows a wooden crane with an unusual wooden cover. Note the workman in the foreground with cord tied round his trouser legs below the knees. This was common practice at the time amongst rural workers, as self-protection against any rats that one might disturb.*

*The same scene sixty years later, c.1955, shows how trade on the canal had gone, resulting in dereliction. It may be noted that before closure, however, the crane had been replaced.*
Photo by F. Blampied.

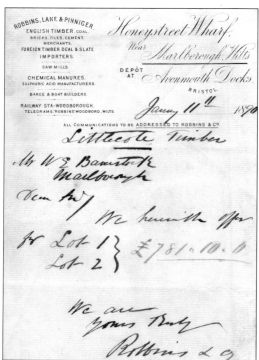

Robbins Lane and Pinniger traded heavily in timber both local and imported. This tender document dated 1890, offered by Robbins Lane and Pinniger, is addressed to a Mr Barnstock of Marlborough for timber from the Littlecote Estate.

Robbins Lane & Pinniger built four main types of boat: the Kennet Barge (70ft x 13ft 10in), narrow boats (70ft x 6ft 10in), the Mule or wide boat (70ft x 10ft) and Severn trows, which had to be no bigger than the barge due to lock sizes. This busy scene from about 1920 shows in the foreground a barge, probably one of the fleet built for United Alkali, two narrow boats, possibly the Kate and the Jane traded by RL&P, and finally a Kennet Barge, which would have been the Unity. From the collection of P.A.J. Brown.

*This painting by Joseph Barnard Davis from c.1860 is important insofar as it depicts the precise layout of the Robbins Lane and Pinniger businesses on both sides of the canal.*

*The recently launched barge* Diamond, *c.1930, built for United Alkali Bristol. The clock from the clock tower can be seen today in full working order hanging in the boiler room at Crofton pumping station.*

*The canal was cut past Wilcot c.1805, through land owned by Mrs Susannah Wroughton. Mrs Wroughton was paid 200 guineas and provided with this ornamental bridge with a landscaped lake on the eastern side as compensation for the canal passing through her land.*

*As the canal fell into disuse, the boats brought over from Wales as mud boats in the 1930s decayed where they were moored. This one at the eastern exit from the Wilcot ornamental lake finally disappeared in 1998. Photo by J.E. Manners.*

James Dredge, engineer and one-time brewer, was born in Devizes in 1794 and moved to Bath with his family in 1822. This suspension bridge, erected in 1845, was designed by Dredge to an order by Col Wroughton to link lands at Stowell (formerly West Towell) west of Pewsey. It is a rare example of his work. The angle of the deck hangers is characteristic of Dredge's designs, the implications of which remain open to debate. Many of his designs were influenced by observations of the natural world.

The Leviathan was a steam powered trip boat built by the Crofton branch of the Kennet & Avon Canal Trust during canal restoration. Based at Pewsey, it can be seen that it was coping with a blanket of weed west of there in 1977. Photo by Philip Wilson.

The paddleboat Charlotte Dundas comes through the road bridge at Pewsey Wharf c.1975. The late Tom Hams, last skipper of the barge Unity, once told how Unity, under tow by two horses which always worked together, was approaching this bridge when the hames of the smaller lead horse caught the masonry, throwing first one and then the other horse into the canal. The wide boat at the wharf belonged to the Dorset Association of Youth.

PWY.114  THE CANAL, PEWSEY WHARF, PEWSEY

Pewsey wharf was owned by the canal company and that ownership has passed through to British Waterways today. The warehouse still stands but there remains no evidence of the crane that once stood here. A company agent and toll collector were once stationed here, although Pewsey lies three quarters of a mile to the south. As a rural wharf, trade inevitably involved grain and flour. Other general goods included coal ashes for roads, coal, timber, gravel and provisions.

*The steam narrow boat* Leviathan *leaves Wootton Rivers lock on one of her regular two-hour cruises to Cadley lock and back. Photo by Philip Wilson.*

*In July 1938 the railway sidings across the canal from Burbage wharf were still in use, although the wharf crane indicates that the once flourishing trade in local timber from the Savernake Forest by canal had stopped. Photo by M.F. Yarwood.*

As the barge Unity enters the eastern portal of the 502 yard (459m) Bruce Tunnel on the summit pound, the horse is led away and over the top. Boats were hauled through the tunnel by hand using a fixed chain on the south wall. Originally this was to have been a deep cutting but it became a tunnel at the insistence of the Earl of Ailsbury, one of the original members of the Canal Committee and through whose lands the canal was to pass. The signal box of the old Savernake station can just be seen top right.

It was William Jessop's report of 1794 which resulted in a short summit pound and a pumping station at Crofton. Two steam driven pumps, which, on steaming weekends, still perform their original task, were installed at Crofton to pump water from Wilton Water to the summit. But by 1955 the canal was no longer navigable and the bed can be seen to be dry. Photo F. Blampied.

In 1958 the boiler stack at Crofton had to be reduced in height for safety reasons but the effect on boiler draught meant that the engines were retired. The pumps and building were bought by the Kennet & Avon Canal Trust, however, and fully restored, with an electric fan installed to boost boiler draught. This photograph was taken during canal restoration. The chimney has now been restored to its original height with funds raised by the trust's 'Buy a Brick' appeal and a major contribution from the Manifold Trust.

A welcome break for photographs at Crofton during restoration. Mentioned by Sir Anthony Durant in his foreword to this book, General Sir Hugh Stockwell is seen on the left of the photo with Arabella. Admiral Sir William O'Brien is seen on the right with Dudley. Other members of this group of eight volunteer restorers are clustered behind Brian Marson, centre foreground. Photo by Terry Fincher.

*A Lancashire boiler at Crofton pumping station in pristine condition after restoration by volunteers.*
Photo by Derek Pratt.

*Volunteers worked hard to restore the pumps and the building to the condition seen here in the cylinder head room. A dedicated team today continues with this work, preserving the expertise necessary to maintain these beautiful examples of past engineering.* Photo by Derek Pratt.

*Here on the driving platform at Crofton in the 1920s, William (Bill) Giles works the handles on the valve levers which have to be operated manually when starting and stopping the engine. Bill was the father of Ethel Giles who, in memory of her parents, set down in a booklet her memories of life at Crofton in the 1920s. (That booklet remains available through Trust outlets.)*

*The* Leviathan *again, this time advertising its presence as it winds on the summit pound* c.1977. Photo by Waterway Productions Ltd.

876

Browmy

Dee 22

**NOT TRANSFERABLE.**                    TICKET NO. 891

## LITTLE BEDWYN CANAL FISHING.

Fishing is permitted between 7.30 a.m. and 7 p.m., by tickets which are issued at 5/- per day on Sunday and 2/6 per week day, from the Tow Path side of the Kennet and Avon Canal East of Burnt Mill Lock, in the Parish of Little Bedwyn, adjoining land owned or occupied by E. B. Gauntlett, Little Bedwyn, Wilts.

Fishing in the stream adjoining the canal and fishing in the canal on the side which the stream is situated is strictly prohibited.

Tickets are issued from the 15th June to 15th March.

Pike fishing to commence September 1st and end January 31st.

Perch fishing is not permitted after January 31st.

No person may use more than **one rod at one time.**

No person may fish within ten yards of another without the permission of the first comer.

Fish under the following sizes to be returned to the water dead or alive : Pike 24 inches, Trout 15 inches, all other fish 8 inches.

The use of trimmers, night lines, bank runners and gorge bait is prohibited.

Tickets are obtainable at "Kelston," Little Redwyn, or at Little Bedwyn Estate Office.

Tickets must be produced on request. Any person found fishing without a ticket or contravening other regulations is liable to prosecution and prohibited from future fishing in the Water.

Issue of tickets may be withdrawn without notice.

Name................................................                    Date....................

*As trade on the canal declined, the value of the waterway for leisure pursuits was recognised. A minority interest at the turn of the century, today leisure activities are dominant. Fishing is one such activity; this book of fishing tickets was issued on 22 December 1944 for a stretch of canal through land owned by Mr E.B. Gauntlett.*

# *Three*
# Froxfield Wharf to the River Thames (Berkshire)

The Wiltshire boundary ends here at Froxfield Wharf and the Berkshire section begins at Froxfield Bridge beside the wharf. Many of those who enjoy the canal today, in whatever capacity, maintain that there is a subtle change at about this point as Hungerford is approached. No one can quite define it, but it probably results from a combination of things, including the changes in architecture, local accents and attitudes.

*Little remains today but a widening of the canal to indicate that there was once a wharf here at Froxfield, sandwiched between the railway, only a few yards away, and the canal. The main A4 trunk road runs close by, to the north of the railway, with Froxfield itself lying just within Wiltshire. In the background can be seen Froxfield lower lock.*

## GREAT WESTERN RAILWAY.

# KENNET & AVON CANAL.

# NOTICE OF STOPPAGE!

**NOTICE IS HEREBY** given that the Water will be withdrawn from the Canal at the

## Cobbler's Lock

in HUNGERFORD MARSH, on Monday, the 9th and Tuesday the 10th of September next, (both days inclusive) for Repairs to the Lock, during which time the Traffic through the Lock will be suspended.

**CHARLES F. HART,**

*Canal Engineer.*

Engineer's Office, Devizes,
28th August, 1889.

*The GWR Act No.1 of 1852 transferred ownership of the canal to GWR, along with a responsibility for maintenance of navigation. It is fair to say that GWR honoured (if at times only just) that requirement. When nationalised in 1948, the canal was still navigable. This notice of intended maintenance in 1889 at Cobblers Lock, west of Hungerford, is a small piece of evidence of that upkeep. What company today would continue to maintain a subsidiary that was losing money?*

*The area around Hungerford is one of rural tranquillity. A lovely stretch of waterway runs through Cobblers Lock, across the marshes, bisects this lovely town and then crosses the Common. Here it is depicted in isolation near the swing-bridge, c.1910.*

*Use of the 'Archimedes screw pump' (or Cochlea) was first reported by Archimedes following a visit to Egypt c.220BC, where he witnessed its use for irrigation. Between that time and the capture of this scene in 1909 it appears to have changed little. It is simply a helix fixed within a tube, the whole being able to rotate. It is being used here to drain an excavated culvert during repairs to the canal outside Hungerford Church.*

*Hungerford wharf was still in use in 1908, although looking somewhat neglected. The horse belonging to the moored barge can just be seen on the wharf in the middle ground.*

Cassells Gazetteer *carried this photograph of Hungerford wharf in 1896. These were reasonably busy times, with trade in local timber.* From the collection of Sue Hopson.

*Another view of the end of Hungerford Wharf looking west c.1900, this time including the lock. The lock appears to be full and a boat is ready to exit, but it has been deserted by the crew.*

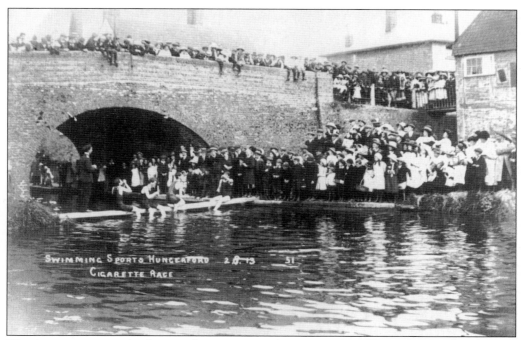

*The cigarette race was clearly a popular event; part of a greater gala at Hungerford Road Bridge, it is shown here in August 1913.*

A rare shot of a Kennet barge under tow and heading east away from Hungerford road bridge. The horse is in the shadow of the footbridge.

The barge Betty owned by H. Dolton & Son, a well-known trader in Newbury, is being loaded with grain at Kintbury wharf c.1908. The wharf was opposite the Dundas Arms below the lock. From the collection of G. Collier.

*Kintbury wharf c.1898; like so many of the rural wharves, it had a steady trade in local timber. The traction engine seen here is using coal, the energy source of the age, to provide steam power for a saw bench and a machine for sharpening one end of fence stakes. The Dundas Arms Hotel had not yet acquired the porch seen in the previous photograph of 1908. From the collection of Sue Hopson.*

*By 1955, just seven years after nationalisation, there was no way that the lower gates of Higgs Lock would hold water.*

*The barge* Betty *owned by H. Dolton & Son ascends through Newbury Lock c.1905. The lock cottage no longer exists.*

*The narrow boat* Columba, *owned by John Knill, at West Mills wharf in Newbury, after carrying salt from Middlewich, Cheshire in February 1950.*

*Just above Newbury lock in 1946, the GWR No.2 maintenance boat is loaded with new gates for Wire Lock. 'Bert' Pirouet leads the hauling gang. The photographer's hob hangs loosely from the hauling line. He was the late John Gould, whose court action against the Government initiated the movement to save the Canal from closure.* Photo John Gould.

*West Mills swing-bridge Newbury c.1905 with weavers' cottages on the right.* From the collection of M. Ware.

*Wide boats moored above Newbury lock c.1920. The boat in the foreground with the abandoned appearance is* Defiance, *owned by canal trader Ferris whose name is also on the empty boat immediately above the lock.* From the collection of M. Ware.

*Two unidentified wide boats moored above Newbury lock. The only means of dating this photograph is by the dress of the lady on the outer boat. A wide-brimmed black hat and a white apron over dark, possibly black, clothing suggest a date of around 1905.*

In the early 1950s, John Knill and John Gould were the main traders keeping the canal alive. Here in 1952 John Knill is delivering grain at West Mills wharf above Newbury lock. West Mills was purchased by Hovis in 1921 but was finally demolished in 1972 to make way for flats.

This view of West Mills wharf looking east was certainly taken pre-1867, probably around 1865. The properties backing the wharf were weavers' cottages. The narrow boat at the wharf waits with a cargo of coal, possibly from the Somerset coalfields.

*A sight of commercial activity, rarely seen on any canal in recent years. This was a working boat rally, which took place at Newbury Wharf on 29 July 1995.*

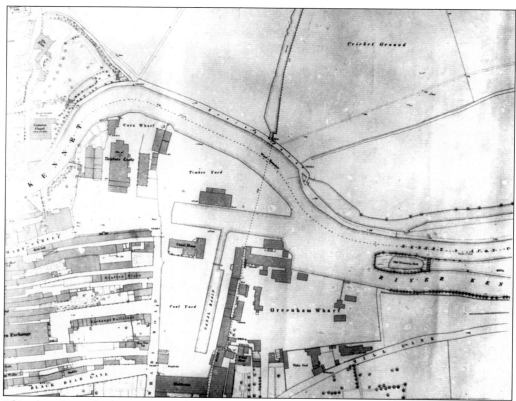

*This plan shows the basins at Newbury wharf in 1880. These, sadly, have now been filled in but a part of the buildings shown on the top left is now known as The Stone Building and is leased to the Kennet & Avon Canal Trust by British Waterways (BW).*

The stone building on Newbury wharf beside the river Kennet was once a warehouse and latterly a canal workshop. It used to be part of a much bigger complex. The 1880 plan shows that what is left today is only a quarter of the original building as evidenced by the brickwork on the south-west corner. The huge girders and central pier of Parkway Bridge spanning the canal can be seen to the right. This bridge was erected in 1940 by GWR as a wartime supplement to Town Bridge and the girders were brought from Maidenhead where they had been intended for use in the abandoned bypass project. It restricted headroom for canal traffic to seven feet at moderate river levels, until spring 2001 when it was raised.

A wintry scene at Newbury wharf with the boat Mate lying alongside c.1910. The typical Kennet & Avon wooden crane would appear still to have been in use.

The narrow boat Hesperus owned by Lord Bingham (father of the disappeared Lord Lucan) heads upstream into Newbury lock towing a landing craft. This photograph was taken in 1948 as Lord Bingham navigated the Kennet & Avon delivering this landing craft to Newbury from Twickenham for Mr Hamblin. The Hesperus continued the journey to Bristol, Sharpness, Manchester, the Trent and Mersey Canal, the Trent, Fossdyke and Witham navigations, Boston, across the Wash and back to the canal system via the River Nene. The crew for the journey was George Day who cleverly wrote the log of the transit of the Kennet & Avon in rhyming verse. George Day had previously taken the 30ft converted lifeboat Tudor Rose through the Canal west to east.

A view looking west of Newbury Bridge framing the entrance to the lock. The river Kennet enters the scene on the right just beyond the pilings between the bridge and the lock gates. This bridge replaced an earlier wooden structure in 1769 and was therefore in existence when building of the canal commenced in 1794. Until this time, Newbury had been the limit of navigation inland from Reading. There was no room for a safe towing path because the waterway was to take barges up to 13ft 10in in the beam. Boatmen therefore had to moor their craft at about this spot and float a tow rope attached to a wooden float from the lock. A nearby notice warned boatmen that they would be fined if they hauled across the road.

*Newbury wharf timber yard is pictured in the early years of this century. The building on the extreme left is today Newbury Museum. Also visible is the river overspill weir.* From the collection of M. Ware.

*This picture from 1932 captures two Swansea Canal boats, part of the fleet of Welsh boats brought down to act as mud boats during the 1930s dredging programme. They are seen lying in the south-east corner of the inner basin (now filled in) at Newbury wharf, just across the coalyard from the weighbridge. The gentleman on the right is Mr Smith, the weighbridge attendant and time-keeper for the coalyard.*

*John Gould's pair of narrow boats* Colin *and* Iris *arrive at Newbury in the winter of 1949. John Gould and John Knill were effectively prevented from carrying on further up the Kennet & Avon Canal on 31 May 1950, when it was closed by the padlocking of lock gates and swing-bridges around Newbury and by the closure of the canal from Burghfield lock to Heales lock. The concrete 'Dragons Teeth' in the park were yet another example of attempts to stop Herr Hitler's tanks in the event of invasion during the Second World War. Following a report in the* Daily Telegraph *in December 1954 that the British Transport Commission intended to close the Kennet & Avon from Reading to Bath, John Gould and Willow Wren Carrying Co. both initiated High Court action against the BTC. This, in effect, resulted in the BTC's intention being thwarted. By 1958 an independent inquiry investigating the future of inland waterways under the chairmanship of Mr Leslie Bowes reported that the Kennet & Avon was a case for redevelopment.*

*John Gould approaches Bulls lock with* Colin *and* Iris *in 1950. The River Kennet re-enters the navigation in the background.*

*An abandoned British Transport Commission dredger at Thatcham in May 1955. A few years later it was inspected by a firm of civil engineers on behalf of the Kennet & Avon Canal Trust in the hope of bringing it back into use. By this time, however, it was beyond resurrection.* Photo by F. Blampied.

*Winding at Longbridge wharf, Thatcham in 1951, with John Gould at the helm.*

*A girl in cape and bonnet picks flowers below Monkey Marsh turf-sided lock c.1905. Photo R. White.*

The narrow boat Hesperus, owned by Lord Bingham, locking up in what was then a turf-sided lock at Woolhampton in 1948. The tow-line to the landing craft being delivered to Newbury can just be made out. Following this epic journey through the Kennet & Avon Canal and the long round trip described earlier the boat was acquired by John Knill. He sold it on to Tom Foxon in 1953. This was Tom Foxon's first boat as a No.1; he renamed it New Hope, after completing National Service.

Aldermaston swing-bridge as it was before the 1950 closure of the canal, which resulted in its decay. It was replaced during restoration by an electrically operated bascule bridge. From the collection of M. Ware.

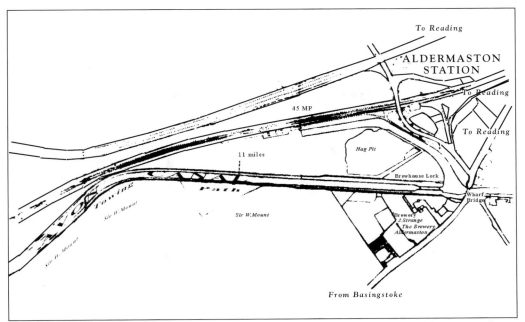

Around the time of the canal takeover by GWR in 1852, the canal company had planned an exchange arm at Aldermaston. Shortly after 1852 this was put into effect, with an additional railway siding. This map shows the layout c.1880, though only a small section of the arm exists today. The curious amongst us can however still trace the course of the railway siding and its arch in the road bridge.

This building pictured c.1950 on the south side of the canal at Aldermaston is the old malthouse. It occupies a position alongside Aldermaston wharf just east of the swing-bridge. The main items of trade from this wharf were timber and locally made timber products. GWR also created a maintenance wharf on the opposite side of the canal.

111

*The scene at Padworth lock with broken lock gates in 1952, prior to restoration, was not encouraging. The use of unsuitable Oregon pine in some new lock gates resulted in their soon requiring replacement.*

*Towney lock, turf-sided as once were all locks on the River Kennet, pictured in 1955. It was clearly going to need considerable attention during any restoration project.*

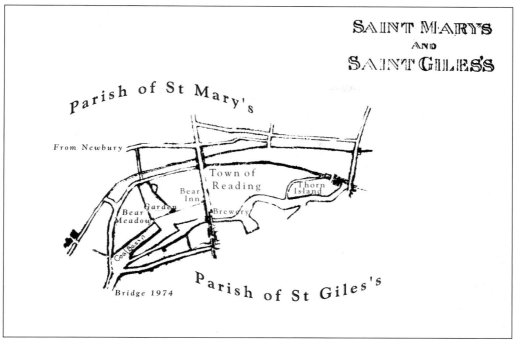

SAINT MARY'S
AND
SAINT GILES'S

Parish of St Mary's

From Newbury

Town of
Reading

Bear
Inn

Thorn
Island

Bear
Meadow

Garden

Brewery

Coal Basin

Bridge 1974

Parish of St Giles's

*This plan of the 'Town of Reading' dates from c.1850 and shows the course of the River Kennet. An interesting feature is the coal basin at 'Bear Meadow'; the absence of County lock is also notable.*

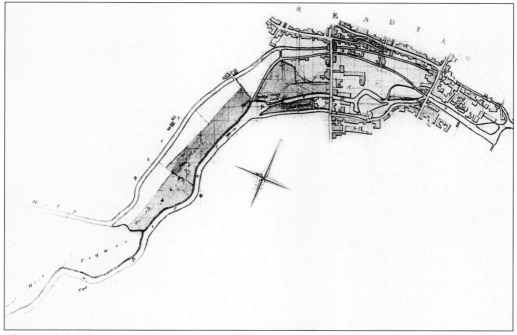

*This is a slightly later map with no coal wharf; County lock has now appeared.*

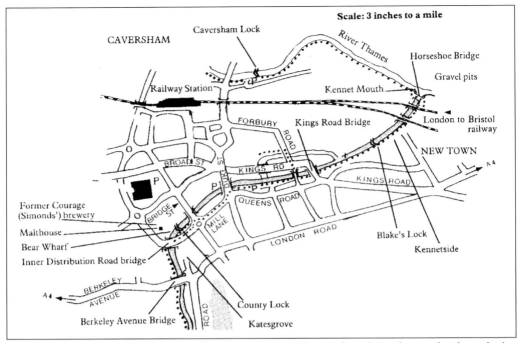

*These two maps show where the main wharves on the River Kennet through Reading used to be and other features referred to in the text; to identify features on the river today these more recent drawings are necessary.*

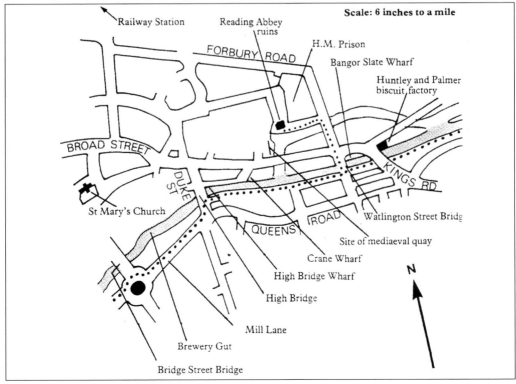

114

*These two coal boats are tied facing up river at Bear Wharf, c.1965.*

Snipe *and* Grebe *leaving County lock in 1950. The boats formed part of the Kennet Carrying Co. owned by Ran Meinertzhagen.*

Enterprise *pictured c.1958 leaving County lock heading up river. This boat formed the basis of Ran Meinertzhagen's Enterprise Cruises.*

*Looking across the river from Bear Wharf, Reading towards County lock in 1961. This was a time when the wharf was still served by rail sidings.*

The approach to County Lock looking downstream. This marks the beginning of the infamous 'Brewery Gut', created when Simonds Brewery bought up the towpath between Bridge Street Bridge and High Bridge in the mid-1880s so that they could build on the land. This forced the river into a deep, narrow, dangerous channel without a tow path, forcing boatmen to float long tow-lines down river. This was a dangerous practice especially when boats met mid-way and accidents did happen. When the canal was restored, traffic lights were installed but the sign in the photo states 'Traffic lights out of order proceed with CAUTION'.

The river is prone to fast flood conditions when it can become unnavigable, as seen here in 1961. The scene is being surveyed by David Blagrove, canal carrier, historian and author.

*The steam launch Sabrina is pictured here in September 1989 above County lock during an eventful trip which resulted in a tow off a shallow section. Owned at this time by Tony Cundick, Crofton restorer, around 1905 it had been owned by the Gloucester Docks Co. who used it as their launch and as a passenger trip boat.*

*The 40ft sailing barge Cygnet aground on the shoal above Bridge Street Bridge in August 1962.*

*Travelling through Brewery Gut in 1997, glimpses of the industrial past witnessed by the working boatmen still lingered.*

*A drawing of Crane Wharf, Reading, by N.H.J. Clarke c.1920. From the collection of J. Edwards.*

*Huntley and Palmer's biscuit factory below King's Road Bridge, Reading, c.1965. Factory jetties were busy until the end of the Second World War unloading flour, trading biscuits to London or receiving Midlands coal delivered by Barlow's boats.*

*The preferential use of the waterways by Huntley & Palmer is confirmed by this logo, once found on some of their biscuit packets. There was less wastage due to breakages with water transport than with land transport and it was cheaper.*

*Looking west from Blakes lock c.1975. This is the last lock on the river Kennet, although not under the control of British Waterways.*

*This is a Maid Line motor cruiser rally at Reading in April 1956. Photo F. Blampied.*

*Jack James' narrow boat Jack seen here at Kennet Side, Reading in 1923. Jack James was a well-known carrier around Reading, the Oxford Canal and the Grand Union.*

*This sketch from c.1845 shows boats on the River Kennet just up river from its junction with the Thames. This bridge carried the Reading, Guildford & Reigate railway.*

*Travelling upriver on the Thames, Kennet mouth is easily missed, but for the boatmen of the past with towing horses this was not a problem. The tow path can be seen on the left as it turns into the Kennet; just a few yards beyond was the ferry, later Horseshoe, Bridge.*

*Just inside Kennet mouth from the Thames is Horseshoe Bridge. When the canal link between Newbury and Bath was completed in 1810, a ferryman was appointed to take towing horses across the mouth of the Kennet. The toll was 2d but in 1892 GWR had this bridge built for horses and pedestrians.*

Bill Chivers was one of the best known traders on the Kennet & Avon Canal and was certainly trading up to 1934 between Reading and Newbury with the barge Marjory. He formed a company with Jack James and Jack Garner – Thames Transport – but when that collapsed in the 1930s he continued

*trading on his own. He was a general carrier and was even known to dredge gravel from the bed of the River Kennet. This venture at Reading, Thames Side, dates from about 1913.*

*The provenance of this photograph links it with the previous; it would appear again to be Thames Side. Once owned by Henry Bright of Newbury, now owned by Chivers, Perseverance is apparently taking on logs from the Chivers operation. This is a fascinating photograph, displaying a number of interesting features. The boat evidently saw much river use, most likely on the*

*Thames and the Kennet. Note the crude extension of the rudder to gain improved steerage. This was probably useful when travelling with the current and steerage way was minimal. Note also the stone on the roof tied to a rope. This would have been used as a light brake to maintain control when travelling downstream and as a mud anchor.*

# Acknowledgments

The authors, on behalf of the Kennet and Avon Canal Trust, wish to acknowledge all those who have been generous enough to provide originals or copies of photographs for use by the trust and for retention in the museum archive. Recognition has been given in the text where individuals have been identified but it is appreciated that many remain anonymous. The trust is grateful to all contributors. The authors have acted as volunteers in the compilation of this book and waive all rights to any revenue from sales, such revenue being paid to the trust in the interest of the canal.